Life Around the World

What Are Holidays Like
Around the World?

By Kathleen Connors

Cavendish Square
New York

Published in 2022 by Cavendish Square Publishing, LLC
243 5th Avenue, Suite 136, New York, NY 10016

Copyright © 2022 by Cavendish Square Publishing, LLC

First Edition

No part of this publication may be reproduced, stored in a retrieval system, or transmitted in any form or by any means—electronic, mechanical, photocopying, recording, or otherwise—without the prior permission of the copyright owner. Request for permission should be addressed to Permissions, Cavendish Square Publishing, 243 5th Avenue, Suite 136, New York, NY 10016. Tel (877) 980-4450; fax (877) 980-4454.

Website: cavendishsq.com

This publication represents the opinions and views of the author based on his or her personal experience, knowledge, and research. The information in this book serves as a general guide only. The author and publisher have used their best efforts in preparing this book and disclaim liability rising directly or indirectly from the use and application of this book.

All websites were available and accurate when this book was sent to press.

Library of Congress Cataloging-in-Publication Data
Names: Connors, Kathleen, author.
Title: What are holidays like around the world? / Kathleen Connors.
Description: New York : Cavendish Square Publishing, [2022] | Series: Life around the world | Includes index.
Identifiers: LCCN 2020031845 | ISBN 9781502659484 (library binding) | ISBN 9781502659460 (paperback) | ISBN 9781502659477 (set) | ISBN 9781502659491 (ebook)
Subjects: LCSH: Holidays–Juvenile literature.
Classification: LCC GT3933 .C63 2022 | DDC 394.26–dc23
LC record available at https://lccn.loc.gov/2020031845

Editor: Kristen Nelson
Designer: Tanya Dellaccio

The photographs in this book are used by permission and through the courtesy of: Cover Kristin F. Ruhs/Shutterstock.com; p. 5 Rawpixel/iStock/Getty Images Plus/Getty Images; p. 7 Deagreez/iStock/Getty Images Plus/Getty Images; p. 9 OLIVIER MORIN/AFP via Getty Images; p. 11 View Stock/Getty Images; p. 13 CARL DE SOUZA/AFP via Getty Images; p. 15 (top) Instants/E+/Getty Images; p. 15 (bottom) hadynyah/E+/Getty Images; p. 17 Eyepix/NurPhoto via Getty Images; p. 19 Hemant Mehta/Canopy/Getty Images Plus/Getty Images; p. 21 J S Jaimohan/Moment/Getty Images Plus/Getty Images; p. 23 M_a_y_a/iStock/Getty Images Plus/Getty Images.

Some of the images in this book illustrate individuals who are models. The depictions do not imply actual situations or events.

CPSIA compliance information: Batch #CS22CSQ: For further information contact Cavendish Square Publishing LLC, New York, New York, at 1-877-980-4450.

Printed in the United States of America

CONTENTS

Time to Celebrate! 4

Marking Special Times 10

Bringing People Together 16

Words to Know 24

Index 24

Time to Celebrate!

Holidays are important days people **celebrate** around the world. They can be just one day or many days. Certain foods may be made. Other **traditions**, such as giving gifts, may be part of a holiday too.

Christmas is celebrated all over the world. Having a Christmas tree is a big part of the holiday in many places. In Ukraine, Christmas trees are covered in spider webs! They're said to bring good luck.

Many people around the world also celebrate on Christmas Eve. This is the day before Christmas. Visiting the **graves** of loved ones is part of celebrating Christmas Eve in Finland. This helps families remember those who have died.

Marking Special Times

The **Lunar** New Year is celebrated in China and throughout Asia. It's not celebrated on the same days every year, but it's commonly in January or February. People wear red for this holiday. It's a lucky color!

The **parades** of Brazil's Carnival celebration are known all over the world. Carnival is celebrated in February or March. There are colorful clothes and a lot of music and dancing. Carnival celebrations go on for days!

Many holidays around the world welcome spring. Holi is a spring holiday in India and other parts of the world. It's a colorful day! People splash each other with colored water and throw colored powder, or dust.

15

Bringing People Together

At the start of November, Mexican families visit the graves of those who have died. They bring food and flowers to share with the dead. This is called the Day of the Dead, or *Día de los Muertos*.

Diwali is called the festival of lights. It's the biggest holiday in India. Diwali is five days long each November. Families celebrate with lamps and candles. They make tasty food to share. There are fireworks too!

The month of Ramadan is an important time for people who follow Muslim beliefs. They fast, or don't eat, during the day. At the end of the month, they celebrate Eid al-Fitr with a big meal!

There are many holidays celebrated around the world. Different countries and groups celebrate different holidays. However, all holidays are the same in some ways. They all bring families and friends together!

WORDS TO KNOW

celebrate: To do something special or fun for an important day such as a holiday.

graves: The places used for burying people who have died.

lunar: Having to do with the moon.

parades: Events with many people and groups moving down a street by marching or riding in cars or on special vehicles.

traditions: Things that have been done for a long time and passed down over time.

INDEX

C
Christmas, 6, 8

D
Day of the Dead, 16

Diwali, 18

E
Eid al-Fitr, 20

H
Holi, 14

L
Lunar New Year, 10

24